greater grave

jacq greyja

the operating system c. 2018

the operating system print//document kin(d)* projects chapbook

greater grave

ISBN: 978-1-946031-39-6
copyright © 2018 by Jacq Greyja
edited and designed by Lynne DeSilva-Johnson with poetry editor Peter Milne Greiner

is released under a Creative Commons CC-BY-NC-ND (Attribution, Non Commercial, No Derivatives) License: its reproduction is encouraged for those who otherwise could not afford its purchase in the case of academic, personal, and other creative usage from which no profit will accrue. Complete rules and restrictions are available at: http://creativecommons.org/licenses/by-nc-nd/3.0/
For additional questions regarding reproduction, quotation, or to request a pdf for review contact operator@theoperatingsystem.org

This text was set in The Constellation of Heracles, Minion, Franchise, and OCR-A Standard.
Books from The Operating System are distributed to the trade by SPD/Small Press Distribution, with ePub and POD via Ingram, with production by Spencer Printing, in Honesdale, PA, in the USA.

Cover Art uses "Section of the Grizzly Giant, 33 feet in diameter, Mariposa Grove, Mariposa County, Cal," a 1870's stereograph by Carleton Watkins in the public domain, from Watkins' "Pacific Coast" series.

The operating system is a member of the Radical Open Access Collective, a community of scholar-led, not-for-profit presses, journals and other open access projects. Now consisting of 40 members, we promote a progressive vision for open publishing in the humanities and social sciences.
Learn more at: http://radicaloa.disruptivemedia.org.uk/about/

Your donation makes our publications, platform and programs possible! We <3 You.
bit.ly/growtheoperatingsystem

the operating system
141 Spencer Street #203
Brooklyn, NY 11205
www.theoperatingsystem.org
operator@theoperatingsystem.org

greater grave

jacq greyja

"PROGRESS STILL CONTROLS US EVEN IN TALES OF RUINATION." -ANNA TSING	9
CAPITAL SELF: QUIETUDE	11
THE AVENUES	12
TO WRITE THE REFUSAL	13
THE 10TH TIRE ON THE ROAD HOME	14
COMPANY PROPERTY	15
X	16
YOU	17
"POSITIVE"	18
THE WARNING SIGN FROM THE ONE WHO STAYS WARM	19
CHOSEN	21
FISCAL CONSTRAINTS	22
WITHOUT END.	23
WRITTEN BY A WHITE MAN	24
"THE IMPERIAL GLOBAL RAINBOW" - *EMPIRE*, XIII	25
A LIST OF COMMONLY MISSPELLED WORDS:	26
SMELL ME	27
DON'T GIVE THIS TIME TO ANYBODY	28
INCISORS	29
LAUGHTER	30
NOTES	33
ACKNOWLEDGEMENTS	35
POETICS AND PROCESS	36

"PROGRESS STILL CONTROLS US EVEN IN TALES OF RUINATION." -ANNA TSING

wanting to edit this memory   I interject
that I recall feeling not-liberated/but
reverting
back before I dis member

I forgot that I disbelieved in liberation
a forgotten action of adjusted time some time ago/ no
speaking is freedom and movement towards freedom a   nd
microdisembodying my pulsations as I
remember them
now
are not and
could not be or
lead towards freedom

the domination of being free/ the being free/ the truth/ the/ love /for the
love of it/ I just love it:
    repeated in response to a question that cannot carry itself

I am very preoccupied with implicating
my body
in a series of violent movements/
isolating and spreading contamination in cohesion with
a decisively nameless flood/
not the flash or the shall   ow but
the current
and always/

the progress of filling orifices is decidedly the only movement/
when proximity is unthinkable movement becomes you

I am talking about the domination   of being free
the doom of not serving but   administering
several kinds of   untraceable

reactions

CAPITAL SELF: QUIETUDE

a blood oath/bornbrother

my belted ex hale

my tattooed twin

"shhhhhhhhhhh hhhhhh

forget what

cums now or cums

alone"

THE AVENUES

      MUST poised as to kill me   s lo w ly
      fornicating MUST as to cover its clothes on my arms i am
      water rising   wiping out   a lifetime of sight

      breath

              MUST cannot cure paralysis   MUST

              dried out the vacuum

              quiet

                      vacuum

              that implural

             air   bag

                    ofpressed handme-downs

      this very old MUST cooing MUST BE   is littering my   private
      parts
      inside herself

To write the refusal until -- it becomes -- I used to say -- atomized -- but now I want to use a different word....

THE 10TH TIRE ON THE ROAD HOME :

gradually lean in on the break or you will die (*her fingers mold the numbers 1 and 3, a 13*)   dying tooth   swept w the other ghosts   asphalt   and   ghost   petting the   scars   as   wedrive i   overwrap   *careful*

barreling 90 mph on sideroads   unable to see past the windshield herbabyyourbaby dying bubbling of departure still wet in their scent filling tunnels   pushing gas pedals circling the lower half of that middle notsouth grassy underbelly whistling   drinking   *to   make   love   to   what   i can't remember*

I AM COMPANY PROPERTY ON COMPANY PROPERTY I AM BREAKABLE PUNISHABLE ERECTED A COINSLOT IE UNIVERSAL COMPANIONSHIP IS POSSIBLE

X

THIS GATHERING

IS FLOWING

THIS GATHERING

IS PLUNGING

SOME OTHER

CORRODED TENDER

2207 MILES

BENEATH

A DRESS

i called you my family before i knew what to call you

"POSITIVE" : currency of earlydeath watchful year
of the   -cosm   of the inthat   of the   commotion

equipment   oiled   by   relish   and   split   doors
documenting (you): narrow space   or   this program

perpetual warmth yet unaccounted:
a barren coast   drying   a drawer on the coast
los angeles will find you and kill you

thighs shuffle a plastic bag of wet letters we check in
and in   *look*:   cinders chase the smoke trail   eat out
unarticulated bonds   anecdoted city   house of waves

promotional material: preferring to centralize and
offer a face of instability

THE WARNING SIGN FROM THE ONE WHO STAYS WARM

readily ignited with flint
    as one burns at a uniform rate
    (impervious to extinguishing once lit)

there are two types of match: raw match, which burns
slowly, and quick match, which   burns quickly

    how many died
    testing how wide a   wound could sear
    how wide it grows
    when the body is un   counted

collisions

play with sequential growth

    a practice of selective figuring

    command to listen/ instruct to die

    under or as a desk

    a chariot

GHOSEN

a serpent eyes
the back of a hand

spun from voice to
        text to skin

to flay that glinting archive
again/tonight

"my kin without record or rope"

FISCAL CONSTRAINTS

knot *unknown* into
systemic violence
the shapeof maybethree faces

facing

~~internal~~ resurrection-of-coil   diluted not-straight tragedy /
orgasm or inanimate object i am
most likely
electrocuted Found particles

ecstasy:
the shock of finding oneself in skin

again

again

again

was sitting on the floor to write incubation when my son was younger, now, he is 15.

I don't know how I wrote that and somehow I have to write again.

I send you the energy of a new writing, and I want you to write it.

Without end.

I know you can do it.

Thank you for finding me on Twitter during my llama tweets; the reality there is that I was

WRITTEN BY A WHITE MAN

                                            in love w/ h is   singed   mandatory
                                                        removal of

                                            record

this is to unbend

the body/ your body
scratched   into me

dragging my skin   behind
him orus
us
longing for yours

"THE IMPERIAL GLOBAL RAINBOW" - EMPIRE, XIII

out of here   now amorphic   i am   unwillingly or foolishly cavorting to a torched song : The Finding, The Reclaimed, The Refusal   none of which i hear (altho the bodies are said to glitter) the gender mothers strum the finale into several chronicles / stained scrolls also glisten and divine a rapture   wrapping arms through the holes of the anxious   the kinky—   declawed and unskinned/ their blushes boiling a hegemony i cannot pronounce until i can / t h is/ my voice evident— descendant of a climbing trilogy/ a mediated change in steps which favors the living:: the body / the owning / the holding   a meditation strung from ashes   how i cannot know what we've shared i cannot know what i am

a list of commonly misspelled words:
availibility suprisingly sobreity

SMELL ME

THREE HEADS TUCKED BE TWEEN
MY LEGS   OVER AND UNDER
EX POSE CHRONIC INVECTION
W/IN BOUNDS OF ASPHIXIATION
AND   ASSAULT

```
the   one          i am         who is many
the many       staying in    who are many
the many      if i cannot    who         are
watching         protest
                 introducin
                 g my self
```

A CHAMBER OF GRIEVANCES BARK
OUT REMOTE   CLOTHED IN
ASSIGNMENTS
SKIN IS NOT-DECIDEDLY
WOMANSYMPATHETICBLEEDINGH
UNGRYSTRAIGHT

> DON'T GIVE
> THIS TIME
> TO ANY
> BODY

INCISORS

we sniff n follow the forge
    arraigned
    symmetrical
caverns of decomposure

tripping blossomed new scars   i've been disappearing you

return after you're off the books
stained

laughing with your spit /is/ our spit

        circles   militate

shocked out of shock   back into clothes
were we building then?

laughter ♥ from demolition ♥ demolition sparked by oil fire ♥
this building is plaguing ♥ myfamilythebuilding ♥ s ha kin g ♥
laug hing ♥ with us ♥ hom e ♥ c o m e h ome ♥ to bury us ♥

notes

"Progress still controls us even in tales of ruination..."
Title from *The Mushroom at the End of the World: On the Possibility of Life in Capitalist Ruins* by Anna Lowenhaupt Tsing: "... the assumption that the trope of progress is sufficient to know the world, both in success and failure. The story of decline offers no leftovers, no excess, nothing that escapes progress. Progress still controls us even in tales of ruination" (21).

"THE IMPERIAL GLOBAL RAINBOW..."
Title from *Empire* by Michael Hardt and Antonio Negri: "Empire manages hybrid identities, flexible hierarchies, and plural exchanges through modulating networks of command. The distinct national colors of the imperialist map of the world have merged and blended in the imperial global rainbow" (xii-xiii).

Illustrations on pages 7 and 31 from Atalanta Fugiens by Michael Maier. Oppenheim, 1617.

Thank you to Bhanu Kapil, whose virtual/textual winds of resilience never failed to resurrect my will to continue through this project.

Thank you to the journals, projects, and editors who published the first iterations of the following poems:

"*Progress still controls us . . .*"
Apogee Journal: Queer History, Queer Now

fiscal constraints and *written by a white man:*
Columbia Poetry Review: Issue 30

"*THE IMPERIAL GLOBAL RAINBOW*"- *Empire, xiii*
The Nottingham Review: Issue 07

the avenues
Berkeley Art Museum & Pacific Film Archive: Way Bay 2018

acknowledgements

This chapbook would not have come to fruition without the care and support of various Bay Area creative writing communities, especially those surviving within (and often against) its academic institutions. Thank you to my friends and kin for reading and rereading this project as it evolved: Kyle Dill, Lindsay Choi, Christina Svenson, Bonnie Cherry, Orooj-e-Zafar, and many others. I am forever grateful for the time, feedback, and encouragement my poetic mentors gifted to this project and its ongoing processes: Claire Marie Stancek, Maxine Chernoff, and Joshua Jennifer Espinoza.

Tremendous gratitude for Jae Granholm, who helped me integrate the artwork by Maier into this book.

poetics and process: a conversation with jacq greyja and lynne desilva-johnson

Greetings comrade! Thank you for talking to us about your process today! Can you introduce yourself, in a way that you would choose?

Hello. My name is Jacq. I'm a queer jewish//latinx writer/poet from California.

Why are you a poet/writer/artist?

I've been wrestling with this question for the last few weeks, trying to really slam an answer out of myself. The process felt masochistic in the sense that I kept returning to the question and attempting an answer, despite this growing feeling of futility—a feeling of getting further and further away from both the question and whatever self could be made to answer.

I recently found my first journal from 1997 in a formerly inaccessible storage unit filled with family documents. The scan I've included here is from my first entry, which I assume to be the first time I wrote to and for myself (at right).

In a way, it feels antithetical to summarize why I write, in part because the process of writing is always moving, always in flux, always responding to so much stimuli that it is hard to narrow in on a singular motivation. But if thinking about why as relating to a point of origin, I imagine that some of the reasons I write today are probably not too different from whatever reasons I had for writing that first entry— moved by the need to uncover that which is sensed but not seen and not fully known. An impulse to document the witnessing of feeling and that which is gone but still present, looming. A mode of understanding my own confessions. A practice or ritual in cultivating a kind of

8/6/1997

Sometimes
wen I hir my mom
and Dad tacing
I fiull sumthing is long
like ther guwing to get a
D a Vows! But thy neve
do.

vulnerability with myself that might be otherwise overwhelming or nonexistent in my relationships with others.

When did you decide you were a poet/writer/artist (and/or: do you feel comfortable calling yourself a poet/writer/artist, what other titles or affiliations do you prefer/feel are more accurate)?

I've never felt completely comfortable calling myself a poet or writer. I'm drawn towards the term "artist," even if I am unsure about adopting it as a title for myself. There is a (perhaps romanticized) sense of openness in "artist" that connects to my creative process in a way that "poet" has not always captured.

In part because of my (strange and uncomfortable) background in English, I at times felt a glaring distinction between my identity and the title of "poet/writer"—not necessarily from a sense of intimidation, but more from a heavy discomfort with the way that academia can use these terms to create standards for what constitutes creative value. The sense of not-belonging was so integral to my experiences in school—dealing with years of undiagnosed and unsupported mental health issues, dropping out of high school, returning to college as a first-generation transfer student—that I felt a tension in aligning myself with terms that were so consistently weaponized in academia.

Within institutionalized spaces, these terms can contribute to a culture of gatekeeping, further contributing (intentionally or unintentionally) to the silencing, discouraging, and ostracizing of marginalized and underrepresented writers. This is especially discouraging for writers whose work not only diverges from the style and content circulated within those spaces, but also directly confronts the systemic problems that their academic institution benefits from. In recent years, I've grown comfortable calling myself a poet. I think part of that comes from developing a kind of kinship with other poets. It might also come from a kind of exhaustion.

What's a "poet" (or "writer" or "artist") anyway?

Right?

What do you see as your cultural and social role (in the literary / artistic / creative community and beyond)?

I'm not sure. I'm not sure that is for me to decide. I know that it is going to keep changing, and I know it is on me to continually read and listen to the work being done around and far beyond me.

Talk about the process or instinct to move these poems (or your work in general) as independent entities into a body of work. How and why did this happen? Have you had this intention for a while? What encouraged and/or confounded this (or a book, in general) coming together? Was it a struggle?

I've started to notice that poems I eventually see as working together in a collection were usually not written with that intention in mind. They are usually written all together with a sense of urgency: as accumulations of long and manic bursts. During those periods of constant writing, I've really benefited from participating in writing groups (though not all writing groups). It's important for me to feel that I can venture into parts of myself that are messy, uncertain, and almost always coated in trauma. I'm okay with realizing that sometimes I am unable to do this in complete isolation.

There's a lot of uncertainty in this chapbook. It has revealed itself to be filled with the circuitous problems that I had been avoiding— problems that I am sure I am continuing to avoid and would like very much to ignore. The poems in this project signal a series of vulnerabilities that I was largely only willing to examine and re-imagine because of a community of writers that made up a summer poetry workshop a few years ago. I wasn't really close friends with anyone; with the exception of a few poets, I did not stay in contact with anyone after the semester ended. But the atmosphere of being around people who were kind and honest and knee-deep in their own work— of having to revisit and revisit the itch that became a wound that became this chapbook—was integral to the process as a whole.

I returned to the very raw and messy first drafts of these poems after a few months of spending time away. I needed to recover from writing just as much as I needed to write. And that makes a huge difference with editing, too. It's a different kind of re-imagining.

Did you envision this collection as a collection or understand your process as writing or making specifically around a theme while the poems themselves were being written / the work was being made? How or how not?

The shared themes across these poems became clear to me only after I had taken that time to move on and away from them. It's a short collection written under intense circumstances, so I don't think I will be "done" with the questions this collection raises for quite a while. If anything, it has initiated a descent into which I am still lowering myself.

What formal structures or other constrictive practices (if any) do you use in the creation of your work? Have certain teachers or instructive environments, or readings/writings/work of other creative people informed the way you work/write?

Ideally, I like to write as much as possible until I feel like I no longer can. While this "method" has ended up working for me, it really came out of not having any time at all to write. I'm not a daily writer, although I wish that I was one. I don't always have the time or the mental energy. I try to set aside 1-2 times per week that I can write straight through for hours, not allowing myself to go back and edit or revise anything until much later. I want to leave myself with as much as possible. I think part of the motivation for this outpour-method stems from the fear that I won't have another chance in the foreseeable future to sit down and write. I try to get as much as I can, whatever it is, onto the page, leaving bread crumbs for myself for when I have time to open it all up again.

I've also been getting a lot out of listening to music while writing, which I never used to do. It's been helping with getting in that unrestrained flow that has become so important to me.

Speaking of monikers, what does your title represent? How was it generated? Talk about the way you titled the book, and how your process of naming (individual pieces, sections, etc) influences you and/or colors your work specifically.

I'm really awful with titles. I've hardly written anything with titles since Greater Grave. *I'm happy with how they work here, but lately I have not felt that they are for me. I think removing the idea that poems need titles has stimulated me to write more and stop less.*

The title for this chapbook was inspired by the tensions generated between the poems themselves, both in their "finished," collective state and their creation as individual pieces. I felt like I was writing into (fragmented) existence the testimony of erasure. The process of action (writing) and non-action (the unwritable) spun together a doubled erasure in terms of process/intention and content/structure. Greater Grave *is the double negative of speaking that erased and unrecoverable testimony— of something buried, gone and yet growing.*

What does this particular work represent to you as indicative of your method/creative practice, your history, your mission/intentions/hopes/plans?

The work in this book is a part of a historical process of recounting, reseeing, and refeeling. So many authors have discussed how writing is a process of living twice. With trauma and PTSD, it is at first twice, and then it is uncountable. This first book might serve as a kind of anchor or buoy. I might swim out and return again and again, in different directions, all within the same body of water. I might leave and not return for awhile. Either situation has applied to my personal relationship with understanding and reliving trauma: circling one or more epicenters of pain. The writing-through and being-of those circulations are so incredibly interconnected; this book is a part of a living history, of living on and reliving. I don't know how it will take shape in the future, but right now I know it is echoing movements I have been making for a long time. I suppose one goal is to allow myself to return to what is in this book if I feel that I must.

What does this book DO (as much as what it says or contains)?

I'm not sure. I know only fractions of what writing this did to me.

What would be the best possible outcome for this book? What might it do in the world, and how will its presence as an object facilitate your creative role in your community and beyond? What are your hopes for this book, and for your practice?

The best possible outcome would be that it resonates. I always hope that the work I put into the world gives readers encouragement to write the thing they need to write in the way that so much of their writing has inspired me as well. Write back to the poems in this, if it helps. Forget about it, if it helps. Don't even finish reading it if you don't want to or can't. The best possible outcome is for readers to feel that they can honestly engage with it and, by extension, contribute to an intimate culture of reading, responding to, and living through work.

Let's talk a little bit about the role of poetics and creative community in social activism, in particular in what I call "Civil Rights 2.0," which has remained immediately present all around us in the time leading up to this series' publication. I'd be curious to hear some thoughts on the challenges we face in speaking and publishing across lines of race, age, privilege, social/cultural background, and sexuality within the community, vs. the dangers of remaining and producing in isolated "silos."

I've spent so much time pouring into the questions raised throughout this interview that I am now unexpectedly floored. I might have too much to say on this. At the moment, I am caught up in the phrase "speaking and publishing across lines." Who sets these lines? The complicated and normalized hierarchies that operate throughout creative spaces make even the imagining of this binary difficult. I am invested in the need for spaces that offer marginalized writers support networks that would be otherwise out of reach. I am also critical of the ways in which gatekeeping re-emerges even in spaces which seek to offer safety and solidarity. And the image of one "producing" in "silos" is both dystopian and familiar. I spoke earlier about the benefits of having a writing community, however temporary or seemingly artificial, during the process of creating this chapbook. But the process of finding community can be scary and fraught. I think it is important to recognize how writing can be isolating even when we do not want it to be.

Is there anything else we should have asked, or that you want to share?

Not that I can think of. I feel so fortunate to be a part of this cohort and to have worked with The Operating System over the last few months. Thank you for this, and for all of the work that you do.

JACQ GREYJA is a queer jewish//latinx poet from California. Their work has been featured or is forthcoming in *Bettering American Poetry: Volume 2, Apogee, Hold: A Journal, Peach Mgzn, Yes Poetry, Berkeley Poetry Review, Nottingham Review, Columbia Poetry Review,* and elsewhere. Their poetry and collages have been exhibited in "Way Bay: Poetry Assembly" at the Berkeley Art Museum & Pacific Film Archive in Berkeley, CA (2018) and "Not Even: Poets Make Collage" at Bushel Collective in Delhi, NY (2017). Jacq earned their B.A. in English from the University of California Berkeley. They are currently pursuing their MFA in Poetry at San Francisco State University, where they are a recipient of the William Dickey Fellowship in Poetry (2017).

WHY PRINT DOCUMENT?

The Operating System uses the language "print document" to differentiate from the book-object as part of our mission to distinguish the act of documentation-in-book-FORM from the act of publishing as a backwards-facing replication of the book's agentive *role* as it may have appeared the last several centuries of its history. Ultimately, I approach the book as TECHNOLOGY: one of a variety of printed documents (in this case, bound) that humans have invented and in turn used to archive and disseminate ideas, beliefs, stories, and other evidence of production.

Ownership and use of printing presses and access to (or restriction of printed materials) has long been a site of struggle, related in many ways to revolutionary activity and the fight for civil rights and free speech all over the world. While (in many countries) the contemporary quotidian landscape has indeed drastically shifted in its access to platforms for sharing information and in the widespread ability to "publish" digitally, even with extremely limited resources, the importance of publication on physical media has not diminished. In fact, this may be the most critical time in recent history for activist groups, artists, and others to insist upon learning, establishing, and encouraging personal and community documentation practices. Hear me out.

With The OS's print endeavors I wanted to open up a conversation about this: the ultimately radical, transgressive act of creating PRINT /DOCUMENTATION in the digital age. It's a question of the archive, and of history: who gets to tell the story, and what evidence of our life, our behaviors, our experiences are we leaving behind? We can know little to nothing about the future into which we're leaving an unprecedentedly digital document trail — but we can be assured that publications, government agencies, museums, schools, and other institutional powers that be will continue to leave BOTH a digital and print version of their production for the official record. Will we?

As a (rogue) anthropologist and long time academic, I can easily pull up many accounts about how lives, behaviors, experiences — how THE STORY of a time or place — was pieced together using the deep study of correspondence, notebooks, and other physical documents which are no longer the norm in many lives and practices. As we move our creative behaviors towards digital note taking, and even audio and video, what can we predict about future technology that is in any way assuring that our stories will be accurately told – or told at all? How will we leave these things for the record?

In these documents we say: WE WERE HERE, WE EXISTED, WE HAVE A DIFFERENT STORY

- Lynne DeSilva-Johnson, Founder/Managing Editor,
THE OPERATING SYSTEM, Brooklyn NY 2017

SELECTED RECENT AND FORTHCOMING OS PRINT/DOCUMENTS

Ark Hive-Marthe Reed [2019]
A Bony Framework for the Tangible Universe-D. Allen [kin(d)*, 2019]
Śnienie / Dreaming - Marta Zelwan/Krystyna Sakowicz,
(Polish-English/dual-language) trans. Victoria Miluch [glossarium, 2019]
Opera on TV-James Brunton [kin(d)*, 2019]
Alparegho: Pareil-À-Rien / Alparegho, Like Nothing Else - Hélène Sanguinetti
(French-English/dual-language), trans. Ann Cefola [glossarium, 2019]
Hall of Waters-Berry Grass [kin(d)*, 2019]
High Tide Of The Eyes - Bijan Elahi (Farsi-English/dual-language)
trans. Rebecca Ruth Gould and Kayvan Tahmasebian [glossarium, 2019]
I Made for You a New Machine and All it Does is Hope - Richard Lucyshyn [2019]
Illusory Borders-Heidi Reszies [2019]
Transitional Object-Adrian Silbernagel [kin(d)*, 2019]
A Year of Misreading the Wildcats [2019]

An Absence So Great and Spontaneous It Is Evidence of Light - Anne Gorrick [2018]
The Book of Everyday Instruction - Chloe Bass [2018]
Executive Orders Vol. II - a collaboration with the Organism for Poetic Research [2018]
One More Revolution - Andrea Mazzariello [2018]
The Suitcase Tree - Filip Marinovich [2018]
Chlorosis - Michael Flatt and Derrick Mund [2018]
Sussuros a Mi Padre - Erick Sáenz [2018]
Sharing Plastic - Blake Nemec [2018]
The Book of Sounds - Mehdi Navid (Farsi dual language, trans. Tina Rahimi) [2018]
In Corpore Sano : Creative Practice and the Challenged Body [Anthology, 2018];
Lynne DeSilva-Johnson and Jay Besemer, co-editors
Abandoners - Lesley Ann Wheeler [2018]
Jazzercise is a Language - Gabriel Ojeda-Sague [2018]
Return Trip / Viaje Al Regreso - Israel Dominguez;
(Spanish-English dual language) trans. Margaret Randall [2018]
Born Again - Ivy Johnson [2018]
Attendance - Rocío Carlos and Rachel McLeod Kaminer [2018]
Singing for Nothing - Wally Swist [2018]
The Ways of the Monster - Jay Besemer [2018]
Walking Away From Explosions in Slow Motion - Gregory Crosby [2018]
The Unspoken - Bob Holman [Bowery Books imprint - 2018]
Field Guide to Autobiography - Melissa Eleftherion [2018]
Kawsay: The Flame of the Jungle - María Vázquez Valdez
(Spanish-English dual language) trans. Margaret Randall [2018]

OS PRINT DOCUMENT ANNUAL CHAPBOOK SERIES TITLES

CHAPBOOK SERIES 2018 : TALES
Greater Grave - Jacq Greyja; Needles of Itching Feathers - Jared Schlickling;
Want-Catcher - Adra Raine; We, The Monstrous - Mark DuCharme

CHAPBOOK SERIES 2017 : INCANTATIONS
featuring original cover art by Barbara Byers
sp. - Susan Charkes; Radio Poems - Jeffrey Cyphers Wright;
Fixing a Witch/Hexing the Stitch - Jacklyn Janeksela;
cosmos a personal voyage by carl sagan ann druyan steven sotor and me - Connie Mae Oliver

CHAPBOOK SERIES 2016: OF SOUND MIND
*featuring the quilt drawings of Daphne Taylor
Improper Maps - Alex Crowley; While Listening - Alaina Ferris;
Chords - Peter Longofono; Any Seam or Needlework - Stanford Cheung

CHAPBOOK SERIES 2015: OF SYSTEMS OF
*featuring original cover art by Emma Steinkraus
Cyclorama - Davy Knittle; The Sensitive Boy Slumber Party Manifesto - Joseph
Cuillier; Neptune Court - Anton Yakovlev; Schema - Anurak Saelow

CHAPBOOK SERIES 2014: BY HAND
Pull, A Ballad - Maryam Parhizkar;
Can You See that Sound - Jeff Musillo
Executive Producer Chris Carter - Peter Milne Greiner;
Spooky Action at a Distance - Gregory Crosby;

CHAPBOOK SERIES 2013: WOODBLOCK
*featuring original prints from Kevin William Reed
Strange Coherence - Bill Considine; The Sword of Things - Tony Hoffman;
Talk About Man Proof - Lancelot Runge / John Kropa;
An Admission as a Warning Against the Value of Our Conclusions - Alexis Quinlan

DOC U MENT
/däkyəmənt/

First meant "instruction" or "evidence," whether written or not.

noun - a piece of written, printed, or electronic matter that provides information or evidence or that serves as an official record
verb - record (something) in written, photographic, or other form
synonyms - paper - deed - record - writing - act - instrument

[Middle English, precept, from Old French, from Latin documentum, example, proof, from docre, to teach; see dek- in Indo-European roots.]

Who is responsible for the manufacture of value?

Based on what supercilious ontology have we landed in a space where we vie against other creative people in vain pursuit of the fleeting credibilities of the scarcity economy, rather than freely collaborating and sharing openly with each other in ecstatic celebration of MAKING?

While we understand and acknowledge the economic pressures and fear-mongering that threatens to dominate and crush the creative impulse, we also believe that ***now more than ever we have the tools to relinquish agency via cooperative means,*** fueled by the fires of the Open Source Movement.

Looking out across the invisible vistas of that rhizomatic parallel country we can begin to see our community beyond constraints, in the place where intention meets resilient, proactive, collaborative organization.

Here is a document born of that belief, sown purely of imagination and will.
When we document we assert. We print to make real, to reify our being there.
When we do so with mindful intention to address our process, to open our work to others, to create beauty in words in space, to respect and acknowledge the strength of the page we now hold physical, a thing in our hand… we remind ourselves that, like Dorothy: *we had the power all along, my dears.*

THE PRINT! DOCUMENT SERIES
is a project of
the trouble with bartleby
in collaboration with
the operating system

www.ingramcontent.com/pod-product-compliance
Lightning Source LLC
Chambersburg PA
CBHW081340080526
44588CB00017B/2688